Prescription Scriptures

Vol. 2   Protection

(Double Hedges of Protection)

Illustrated by: Sunni Barbosa-Reeves and Tommy Reeves

Prescription Scriptures

(Double Hedges of Protection)

ISBN-13:
978-1718685826

ISBN-10:
1718685823

Thank You for Supporting Positive Media!

These teachings have been inspired by:

Pastor Monique

&

Walter Rice
(World Outreach Christian Center)

May God Himself continue to reward your obedience!
Thank you

This is a book that allows you to save time, in a time of need by taking you straight to the protection scriptures of the Bible without the search. Nothing is too big for God.

All you gotta do is believe.

This is what you will need to do:

Speak in into Existence! These Scriptures are to be recited as many times as needed. (There are no words more powerful then Gods Words, use them to stab and poke holes in the devil's butt! Now, Doesn't that sound like FUN?)

1. Believe! (True Faith) Believing that God is able and will protect you according to His own words.

2. Use your weapons! Understand that the battle and your weapons are not carnal, but spiritual.

3. Instead of always running from the devil try this: STOP, STAND and START a fight with him for a change!

4. Call on the Host of Heaven! GOD created angels specifically to fight on our behalf, and they are just standing by waiting to come against the enemy for our sake, Activate Them Now!!! Say This and mean it! (Matthew 26:53 Thinkest thou that I cannot now pray to my Father, and he shall presently give me more than twelve legions of angels

Ephesians 6:12 For we wrestle not against flesh and blood, but against principalities, against powers, against the rulers of the darkness of this world, against spiritual wickedness in high places.

Therefore;

2 Corinthians 10:4 For the weapons of our warfare are not carnal, but mighty through GOD to the pulling down of strong holds.

What are your Spiritual Weapons???

1. The Word of GOD (Example: memorize your scriptures and use them instead of curse words or your own words, why because the devil laughs at anything other than the Word of GOD!)
2. The Blood of the Lamb (Anointing Oil) buy some olive oil and anoint it! Special prayers for anointing your oil may be found on youtube. (Example: I Pled the Blood of The Lamb over EVERYTHING!!!)
3. The Mighty Name of Jesus (Example: No weapons formed against me shall prosper in the Mighty Name of The Lord Jesus Christ.)

Romans 8:31   What shall we then say to these things? If GOD is for us, who can be against us?

Mark 3:27   No man can enter into a strong man's house, and spoil his goods, except he will first bind the strong man; and then he will spoil his house.

Ephesians 6:11   Put on the whole armour of GOD, that ye may be able to stand against the whiles of the devil.

Psalm 32:7 Thou art my hiding place; thou shalt preserve me from trouble; thou shalt compass me about with songs of deliverance. Selah

Luke 10:19   Behold, I give unto you power to tread on serpents and scorpions, and over all the power of the enemy: and nothing shall by any means hurt you.

Hebrews 4:12   For the Word of GOD is quick, and powerful, and sharper than any two-edged sword, piercing even to the dividing asunder of soul and spirit, and of the joints and marrow, and is a discerner of the thoughts and intents of the heart.

Hebrews 13:6   So that we may boldly say, The LORD is my helper, and I will not fear what man shall do unto me.

Psalm 91:11   For HE shall give HIS angels charge over thee, to keep thee in all thy ways.

Isaiah 54:17   No weapon that is formed against thee shall prosper; and every tongue that shall rise against thee in judgment thou shalt condemn. This is the heritage of the servants of the LORD, and their righteousness is of me, saith the LORD.

Psalm 7:6   Arise, O LORD, in thine anger, lift-up thyself because of the rage of mine enemies: and awake for me to the judgment that thou hast commanded.

Deuteronomy 23:14   For the LORD thy GOD walketh in the midst of thy camp to deliver thee, and to give up thine enemies before thee; therefore shall thy camp be holy: that HE see no unclean thing in thee, and turn away from thee.

Philippians 4:13   I can do all things through CHRIST which strengtheneth me.

Isaiah 46:4   And even to your old age I am HE; and even to hoar hairs will I carry you: I have made, and I will; even I will carry, and will deliver you.

Psalm 34:22   The LORD redeemeth the soul of HIS servants: and none of them that trust in HIM shall be desolate.

Isaiah 1:17   Learn to do well; seek judgment, relieve the oppressed, judge the fatherless; plead for the widow.

Proverbs 30:5   Every word of GOD is pure: HE is a shield unto them that put their trust in HIM.

Psalm 16:8   I have set the LORD always before me: because HE is at my right hand, I shall not be moved.

Romans 8:37   Nay, in all these things
we are more than conquerors
through HIM that loved us.

Psalm 34:7   The angel of the LORD encampeth round about them that fear HIM, and delivereth them.

Made in the USA
Columbia, SC
19 April 2021